Step into Science

What Do We Know Now?

Drawing Conclusions and Answering the Question

Robin Johnson

Science education consultant: Suzy Gazlay

Crabtree Publishing Company

www.crabtreebooks.com

Crabtree Publishing Company

www.crabtreebooks.com

Author: Robin Johnson
Series editor: Vashti Gwynn
Editorial director: Paul Humphrey
Editor: Adrianna Morganelli
Proofreader: Reagan Miller
Production coordinator: Katherine Berti
Prepress technician: Katherine Berti
Project manager: Kathy Middleton
Illustration: Stefan Chabluk and Stuart Harrison
Photography: Chris Fairclough
Design: sprout.uk.com
Photo research: Vashti Gwynn

Produced for Crabtree Publishing Company by Discovery Books.

Thanks to models Ottilie and Sorcha Austin-Baker, Dan Brice-Bateman, Matthew Morris, and Amrit and Tara Shoker.

Photographs:
Comstock: p. 13
Corbis: Yann Arthus-Bertrand: p. 22 (bottom right)
Getty Images: Oli Scarff: p. 4 (bottom left); Antenna:
    p. 14; De Agostini Picture Library: Dea/G. Dagli Orti:
    p. 17 (bottom); Stephen Frink: p. 23; Nicole Hill:
    p. 24, 27 (bottom); S. Lowry/Univ Ulster: p. 25;
    Ariel Skelley: p. 28
Istockphoto: Ktaylorg: p. 18 (right); JBryson: p. 19 (top)
Library of Congress: p. 10 (left)
Samara Parent: back cover, p. 1 (top)
Sam Tygier: p. 15 (top)
Science Photo Library: John Reader: p. 7 (top)
Shutterstock: cover, p. 1 (center left and center right),
    3, 10 (right), 17 (center top), 27 (center top); AVAVA:
    p. 29; Doug James: p. 6; Christopher Halloran:
    p. 8 (bottom); Christos Georghiou: p. 11 (right);
    Joca De Jong: p. 22 (center left)

Library and Archives Canada Cataloguing in Publication

Johnson, Robin (Robin R.)
    What do we know now? Drawing conclusions and answering
the question / Robin Johnson.

(Step into science)
Includes index.
ISBN 978-0-7787-5153-3 (bound).--ISBN 978-0-7787-5168-7 (pbk.)

        1. Science--Methodology--Juvenile literature. 2. Science--
Experiments--Juvenile literature. I. Title. II. Series: Step into
science (St. Catharines, Ont.)

Q175.2.J64 2010   j507.8   C2009-906459-6

Library of Congress Cataloging-in-Publication Data

Johnson, Robin (Robin R.)
 What do we know now? Drawing conclusions and answering the
question / Robin Johnson.
    p. cm. -- (Step into science)
 Includes index.
 ISBN 978-0-7787-5153-3 (reinforced lib. bd.g : alk. paper)
-- ISBN 978-0-7787-5168-7 (pbk. : alk. paper)
 1. Science--Methodology--Juvenile literature. 2. Science--Experiments--
Juvenile literature. I. Title. II. Series.

 Q175.2.J64 2010
 507.8--dc22

                                    2009044171

Crabtree Publishing Company

Printed in the U.S.A./122009/CG20091120

www.crabtreebooks.com   1-800-387-7650

Published in Canada
Crabtree Publishing
616 Welland Ave.
St. Catharines, Ontario
L2M 5V6

Published in the United States
Crabtree Publishing
PMB 59051
350 Fifth Avenue, 59th Floor
New York, New York 10118

Published in the United Kingdom
Crabtree Publishing
Maritime House
Basin Road North, Hove
BN41 1WR

Published in Australia
Crabtree Publishing
386 Mt. Alexander Rd.
Ascot Vale (Melbourne)
VIC 3032

CONTENTS

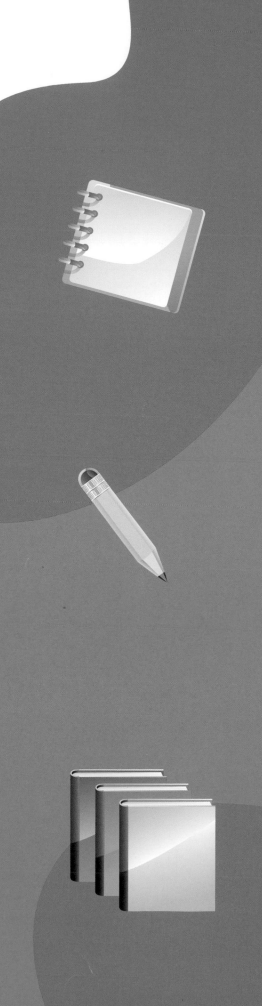

THE SCIENTIFIC METHOD

Have you ever been in an elevator? The scientific method is like an elevator—you enter at the first floor and take the elevator up. The elevator passes one floor at a time, and you get closer and closer to your final stop. Sometimes, however, the journey takes you back down before you continue on to reach your destination.

In the same way, following each step in the scientific method is important for making scientific discoveries. Sometimes, though, scientists have to stop, go back, and think again before they continue.

This book looks at the final step of the scientific method. In it, you will learn how to make **conclusions** from your data. Then you can decide if you proved your hypothesis. You will learn how to communicate the results of your experiment to others. You will also discover how science experiments lead to more questions and more discoveries!

▲ This scientist is recording his observations about a meerkat. He will use the data to make a conclusion.

Beginning Your Scientific Investigation

Be curious! Questions can come from anywhere, anytime. Questions help scientists make **observations** and do **research**. Science is all about problem-solving!

Making Your Hypothesis

So, what is next? You have a question, and you have done some research. You think you know what will happen when you perform your experiment. The term **hypothesis** means educated guess. So, make a guess and get started!

Designing Your Experiment

How are you going to test your hypothesis? Designing a safe, accurate experiment will give **results** that answer your question.

Collecting and Recording Your Data

During an experiment, scientists make careful observations and record exactly what happens.

Displaying and Understanding Results

Now your **data** can be organized into **graphs**, **charts**, and diagrams. These help you read the information, think about it, and figure out what it means.

Making Conclusions and Answering the Question

So, what did you learn during your experiment? Did your data prove your hypothesis? Scientists share their results so other scientists can try the experiment, or use the results to design another experiment.

THE RESULTS ARE IN!

You have completed the first five steps of the scientific method. This means it is time to make conclusions about your experiment. A conclusion is where you determine what your experiment shows.

Carefully read through your notes to see if you answered your experiment's question. Do the results show that your hypothesis was correct? Did you prove what you set out to prove? Why or why not?

Be honest when you analyze your data. Never make up research or conclusions. It is wrong to change or add information and it is not the point of science.

▼ What would happen if the makers of these cars had discovered they were unsafe to drive? What if they had then lied about their conclusions? The drivers would be in for a very dangerous ride!

Take time to make a conclusion, and think hard about your data. Make sure your research really proves—or **disproves**—your hypothesis. To disprove a hypothesis means to show that it isn't true.

The Piltdown Man

In 1912, a scientist named Charles Dawson claimed to have found a very important skull (above). This skull looked a bit like a human's skull, but also a bit like an ape's skull. Scientists hypothesized it was a skull from a very early kind of human. They called it Piltdown Man. No one had ever seen anything like it before. It wasn't until 1953 that everyone realized it was fake. Part of it was an ordinary human skull. But part of it was from a type of ape called an orangutan! Someone had tricked the scientists by sticking the two together! Whoever it was wasted the time of many scientists for years.

GOOD MISTAKES

If the results of your experiment do not prove your hypothesis, don't worry! Look at your data to see what it *does* prove. Some very important discoveries were made by accident!

Make no mistake about it! Sometimes errors lead to important discoveries.

What's Cooking?

In 1945, Percy Spencer was working on radar machines. When he stood near a certain part of the machine, he noticed that the chocolate bar in his pocket melted. Spencer's careful observation led to his invention of the microwave oven.

▼ This man is using a microwave to prepare a quick dinner for his family. Spencer's accidental discovery is now used all over the world.

When you do an experiment properly, and carefully record your results, you will always prove *something*.

For example, perhaps your hypothesis is that heavy objects fall to the ground faster than light objects do. To try to prove your hypothesis, you stand on a chair and drop a tiny pebble and a large, heavy stone at the same time. Both hit the ground at the same time! You repeat the experiment a couple of times. Every time your results are the same.

Your hypothesis was wrong, but you now have evidence of an important scientific fact—that the force of **gravity** pulls all objects down toward Earth at the same speed.

▶ This young scientist is testing her hypothesis about gravity. She knows it doesn't matter if her hypothesis is wrong. She will still reach a useful conclusion.

TRY AND TRY AGAIN

Sometimes if an experiment doesn't go the way you expect, it is not because your hypothesis was wrong. Sometimes it is because the experiment wasn't done properly. If an experiment isn't done properly, it doesn't give true results.

"Anyone who has never made a mistake has never tried anything new."

Scientist Albert Einstein

Great Galileo

Italian scientist Galileo Galilei (left) (1564–1642) proved that the planets circle around the Sun. He also proved that the force of gravity makes all objects fall at the same speed. People did not believe Galileo's conclusions at the time.

So how do you know if you did your experiment properly? Try asking yourself these questions:

- Did I get enough information to prove or disprove my hypothesis?

- Did I change only one **independent variable** at a time?

- Did I make my observations at the same time, or under the same **conditions** each time?

- Was my experiment disturbed by anyone?

- Did my equipment work properly?

After asking those questions, you might realize your experiment wasn't done properly. Then you will need to do the experiment again—and again, if necessary!

▼ Scientists have made many mistakes since they first began studying the world. Early scientists believed that Earth was the center of our solar system. We now know that Earth and other planets revolve around the Sun.

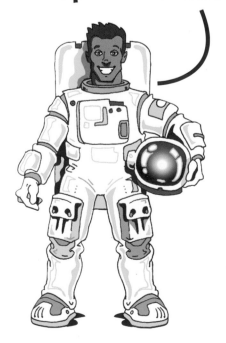

It's not the end of the world if your experiment fails.

LET'S EXPERIMENT!

The Nose Knows

Problem

You might have noticed that things taste different when you have a cold. Why is this? What is it about a cold that makes your favorite pizza taste like cardboard? What do you think? Make a hypothesis.

Materials:

- ☑ three drinking glasses
- ☑ three types of fruit juice
- ☑ paper or a journal
- ☑ a pencil
- ☑ a blindfold
- ☑ a few friends

There is no accounting for taste. Or is there?

1 Blindfold a friend. Make sure he or she doesn't see the different juices first. Ask him or her to taste and identify one type of juice at a time.

2 Now, ask your friend to hold his or her nose and taste the juices again. Was your friend able to tell the juices apart this time?

3 Repeat the **procedure** with several people to make sure the results are accurate.

4 Draw a chart of your results. Make your conclusion. Was your hypothesis correct?

Food for Thought

Has this experiment left you with more questions? Try using fruits, vegetables, and other foods, too. Do you get the same results? Is it easier to identify solid foods than liquids? What happens if you blindfold your friends after they see the foods?

SHARING SCIENCE

When it comes to science, sharing information is very important. Sharing scientific results and discoveries allows people to learn important new things about the world. Science helps people understand why things happen the way they do. It also helps other scientists design new experiments and find out more important things!

▼ These young scientists are working together and sharing their conclusions.

When professional scientists do experiments, they write about their work and try to **publish** it. Before they do so, a few other scientists carefully read and check the report. Then it is published in magazines called **scientific journals** for everyone to read. Scientists also share their results by talking about their work at public scientific meetings. These are called conferences. Conferences happen all over the world for many different types of science.

▶ This scientist is a real pro! He is presenting his research and conclusions to other scientists at a scientific conference.

The Wright Stuff

Orville and Wilbur Wright were American inventors. They worked together to design and build the first powered airplane. The brothers flew the plane at Kitty Hawk, North Carolina, in 1903. What if the airplane had not been invented? How would we travel to faraway places? Think of other scientific discoveries you would miss if they had not been made and shared with the world.

Be like the Wright brothers and let your ideas take flight!

READ ALL ABOUT IT!

A good way to share your results is to write a report. Your report is based on all the notes you made in your **journal**. Your report should provide as much detail as possible. It should explain your experiment clearly and carefully. It should also show how you followed each step of the scientific method. If your journal is neat and complete, writing your report will be much easier.

The first copy of your report might be messy or have mistakes. This is fine! It will help you organize your information before you begin your final copy.

Write or print your report neatly. Don't use fancy letters that are difficult to read. Don't use special effects, or decorate your report with flowers or other designs.

Flower Power Experiment

Question: What do cut flowers do with the water they are put in?
People always put cut flowers in water. This helps them stay fresh for longer. But what do the flowers do with the water they are put in? Where does it go?

Research
I read the book *How Plants Live* by Max Jones. It said that plants take up water through their roots. It goes up the stem and into the leaves and the flowers. Cut flowers don't have roots, but I thought they would still take up water. The water would go up their stems and into the flower heads.

Hypothesis
Cut flowers in water take up water through their stems and into the flower head. This helps them stay fresh longer than a cut flower with no water.

Materials
2 cut white flowers
2 drinking glasses
Water
Red food coloring
A camera

1.
2.

▶ This science report makes the grade! It is neat, clear, and well organized.

3

Write On!

Consider the following questions when writing your report:

• What is the title of your experiment?

• What question did you ask at the beginning?

• What research did you do into your question? Write a list of all the places you found information. This is called a bibliography.

• What is your hypothesis?

• What materials did you use to do your experiment?

• How did you do your experiment? This is called the procedure.

• What **variable** did you change? What variables did you keep the same?

• What observations did you make during your experiment?

• Did you make any changes during your experiment? If you did, why?

• What data did you gather? You can include tables, charts, and graphs.

• What conclusion can you make about your experiment? What did it prove? Was your hypothesis right or wrong?

• Do you have any ideas for more research or experiments?

Spread the word!

▲ Scientists have been reporting their work for hundreds of years. This scientific paper was written in the 13th century by Albertus Magnus. It is about the natural world.

MORE WAYS TO SHARE

There are many other ways to share your scientific conclusions with other people. Use your imagination to come up with interesting ways to tell your friends and family all about your experiments.

The Internet is a valuable tool for sharing information, including science experiments. Ask your parents or teacher to help you find a Web site that allows you to post your experiment. You can also chat with other young scientists about their discoveries. Be sure to visit only Web sites that have been approved by your parents or teachers.

► This girl is surfing for science! She is sharing her scientific discoveries on the Internet—and finding ideas for new experiments, too!

Join the science scene!

Go Clubbing

Join the science club at your school. There, you will meet other curious scientists. They will want to hear all about your experiments. They can also share their own discoveries with you. If your school does not have a science club, ask your teacher if he or she would help you get one started. Or, start your own science club at your home. Invite your friends and family to join your club and discover science with you. The science club members shown above are doing a **chemistry** experiment.

LET'S EXPERIMENT!

Flower Power

Problem

Plants need water. You might have noticed that people put cut flowers in water. What do you think the flower does with that water? Where does it go? Make a hypothesis and then try this experiment.

1 Fill one glass half full with tap water. Add about a capful of food coloring. Leave the other glass empty.

Materials:
- ☑ two freshly cut white flowers
- ☑ two drinking glasses
- ☑ food coloring
- ☑ water
- ☑ journal or paper and pencil
- ☑ colored pencils

2 Put one flower in each glass.

3 Check your experiment every hour to see what happens. Leave it for a week, and see if and how the flowers have changed.

4 Record your observations in your journal. Think about using drawings and color to show your data.

Colorful Conclusions

What did your experiment show? Did you prove or disprove your hypothesis? Write a report to share your results with others. Think about the colorful display you could make, too.

PUTTING IT TO THE TEST

Sharing your results means that other scientists can test your hypothesis. When you make a new discovery, scientists need to be able to repeat your experiment. When they do, they need to get the same results. Then scientists will know that your conclusions are valid, which means true. Sharing data also allows scientists to change parts of the experiment to reach new conclusions.

Is your experiment tried, tested, and true?

Wild About Science

George Schaller studied mountain gorillas by observing them in their **habitats** in Africa. Schaller shared his conclusions—that the animals were gentle and intelligent—in a book published in 1963. Dian Fossey (right) followed Schaller with her own study of mountain gorillas in the wild. Fossey reached similar conclusions and shared them in a book called *Gorillas in the Mist*.

▲ Don't try this at home! This scientist is trained to experiment with sharks—and live to share her results!

Even though scientists repeat each other's experiments, you should always check with a parent or teacher before attempting any experiment on your own. Some experiments are difficult or expensive to do. They might even be dangerous.

For example, Dr. Eugenie Clark spent a long time feeding different types of fish to wild sharks. She believed she could create a shark repellent—and she did! It's a liquid made by a fish called the Moses Sole.

FAIR GAME

Science fairs are a great way for young scientists to meet and share their information. Science fairs are events at which students can show each other their experiments and results. Teachers or other judges sometimes award prizes to students. The judges consider who did the most interesting experiments, and who carefully followed the scientific method. They also look at who has the neatest and clearest display.

Tips of the Trade

- For your science fair display, you will need your journal, your report, and a display board.

- Your display board shows all the important parts of your experiment. Make sure you keep it neat and simple. Too much information can be confusing.

- Be enthusiastic about your experiment. If anyone asks you questions about it, show them that you're proud of your project.

- Do the experiment and make the display yourself. Getting your parents to do the work is just not right! Judges and teachers can always tell if you've had too much help—and they may **disqualify** you for it.

▼ This young scientist is proud of her project. She worked hard to do an experiment and make a neat and organized display.

Hold the Ice!

In 2006, a Florida student named Jasmine Roberts made a science fair project. Her project got her in the news! For her experiment, Roberts got both ice cubes and toilet water from five local fast-food restaurants. Then she tested both for **bacteria**. Bacteria are tiny creatures, like the ones shown magnified below. They often grow in dirt and some kinds of bacteria can make you ill. Roberts discovered that most of the ice had more bacteria in it than most of the toilet water! Yuck! Roberts did win the fair though!

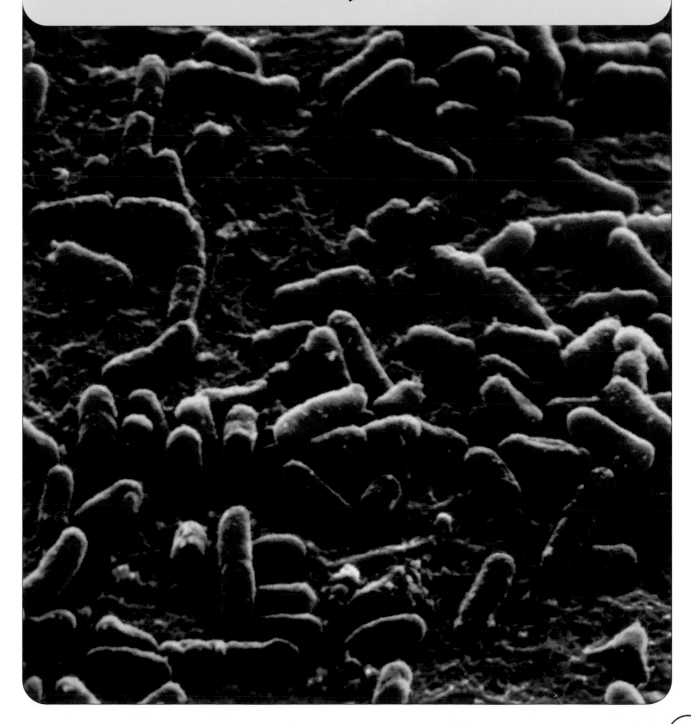

MAKE A SCIENCE FAIR DISPLAY!

Follow these instructions to make a great science fair display!

Use a three-sided board to make your main display. Take a look at the picture of the science fair stand below to see where everything should go. Remember your middle board is the board that people will notice first, so make it look neat and interesting.

▼ This display is neat, colorful, and interesting. The scientist is using some samples from her experiment as models.

Make sure you put your science journal and your report on the table with your board. Then judges, teachers, and other people can find out all the details of your experiment. Your journal should show that you observed your experiment carefully and regularly. Your report can be a single page or several pages in length, but it must be part of your display. You should also include **models** or any parts of your experiment that can be displayed. For example, you could display a variety of flowers that changed color in the flower power experiment from pages 20-21.

Be a science show-stopper! Use your creativity to make your display stand out.

▼ This student has earned a ribbon for his science fair project. He worked hard on his display—and it shows!

NOW WHAT?

So, you had an idea for a science experiment that was pure genius. You did your experiment by carefully following the steps of the scientific method. You shared information about your experiment with other people. Now what do you do?

"To myself I am only a child playing on the beach, while vast (huge) oceans of truth lie undiscovered before me."

Scientist Sir Isaac Newton

▼ This student has made a model of the solar system. She is sharing what she learned with others.

Think about your experiment again. Are there any ways you could change it or make it better? Does it make you wonder about anything else? Perhaps it's given you some more scientific questions?

Sometimes, great inventions and cool discoveries come from past experiments. So don't stop here! Keep on questioning, keep on experimenting, and keep on discovering!

▲ This young scientist is looking at plant cells through a microscope. She knows that everything—no matter how big or small—can be full of wonder.

TIMELINE

Below is a list of discoveries and inventions that were shared with the world.

Year	Discovery or invention	Who made the conclusion and shared the results?
1440	The printing press	Johannes Gutenberg develops the first printing press in Europe. The printing press makes it possible to print books in large numbers, giving scientists a way to share and spread information.
1687	Newton publishes his work	Sir Isaac Newton publishes a book called *The Mathematical Principles of Natural Philosophy*. In the book, Newton uses math to explain how the universe works.
1859	Darwin shares his findings	Charles Darwin publishes a book about **evolution** called *On the Origin of the Species*. Evolution is a process in which animals and plants gradually change and adapt to their habitats.
1872	*Popular Science*	A magazine called *Popular Science* is founded. It publishes articles about scientific discoveries and achievements. It shares the work of many great scientists.
1901	The Nobel Prize	The Nobel Prize is awarded for the first time. The Nobel Prize is given each year to scientists who make and share important discoveries or inventions.
1957	The first science fairs	Students in grades 9 to 12 in the United States begin displaying their experiments in science fairs. Discoveries like Jonas Salk's **vaccine** for a disease called polio make science and science fairs popular.

GLOSSARY

bacteria Living things that are extremely small and sometimes cause disease

chart A way of showing numbers in rows and columns. It is also called a table

chemistry The study of the different types of matter

conclusion What your experiment shows

condition The state something is in

data Scientific information

disproves Shows that something isn't true

disqualify To be removed from a competition for not following the rules

evolution The process by which living things change over time

graph A diagram that can illustrate the results of an experiment. A graph has one measurement along the bottom, and another up the side

gravity The invisible force that pulls objects toward Earth

habitat The natural home of an animal or plant

hypothesis An educated guess about what an experiment might prove

independent variable The thing that you change so that you can see the effect on your samples

journal A record of every step of an experiment

model An object used to show or explain an idea

observation Noticing something happening by using the five senses

procedure The order in which something is done

publish To print something for the public to read

radar A machine that discovers the position and speed of large objects

research Finding out facts about something

results The information that comes from an experiment

science fairs Events at which students display their experiments

scientific journals Magazines that publish important scientific discoveries

scientific method The way to do an experiment properly

vaccine A substance that helps prevent dangerous diseases

variable A part of an experiment that can be changed

FURTHER INFORMATION

Books

101 Great Science Experiments, Neil Ardley, New York: Dorling Kindersley Limited, April 2006

The Wright Brothers' Glider, Crabtree Publishing Company, 2008

Web sites

school.discoveryeducation.com/sciencefaircentral/

www.sciencebuddies.org
Click on the Topic Selection Wizard for science fair project ideas.

INDEX